It's Easy To Play Mozart.

Wise Publications
London/New York/Sydney

Exclusive Distributors:
Music Sales Limited
8/9 Frith Street, London, W1V 5TZ, England.
Music Sales Pty. Limited
120 Rothschild Avenue, Rosebery, NSW 2018, Australia.

This book © Copyright 1988 by
Wise Publications
UK ISBN 0.7119.1523.7
Order No. AM 71754

Art direction by Mike Bell
Cover illustration by Paul Leith
Compiled by Peter Evans
Arranged by Daniel Scott

Music Sales complete catalogue lists thousands
of titles and is free from your local music
book shop, or direct from Music Sales Limited.
Please send a Cheque or Postal Order for £1·50 for postage to
Music Sales Limited, 8/9 Frith Street, London, W1V 5TZ.

Agnus Dei
(Coronation Mass)

Composed by Wolfgang Amadeus Mozart

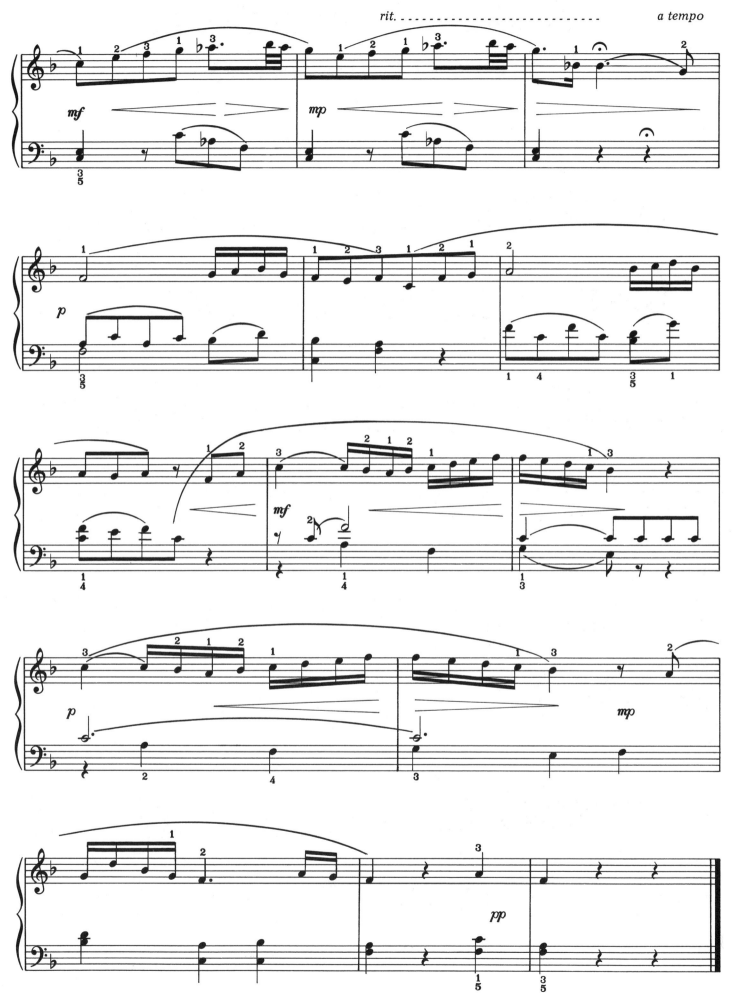

Andante from Sinfonia Concertante K.364

Composed by Wolfgang Amadeus Mozart

9

Eine Kleine Nachtmusik
(Rondo)

Composed by Wolfgang Amadeus Mozart

Minuet In F
K.2

Composed by Wolfgang Amadeus Mozart

Ave Verum

Composed by Wolfgang Amadeus Mozart

Theme from Symphony No.40

Composed by Wolfgang Amadeus Mozart

Romance from Piano Concerto No.20 In D Minor K.466

Composed by Wolfgang Amadeus Mozart

poco cresc.

p

p

p

p

19

Minuet from Don Giovanni

Composed by Wolfgang Amadeus Mozart

Tempo di minuetto

Clarinet Concerto
(Slow Movement)

Composed by Wolfgang Amadeus Mozart

Eine Kleine Nachtmusik (Serenade)

Composed by Wolfgang Amadeus Mozart

Kyrie Eleison

Composed by Wolfgang Amadeus Mozart

29

Theme from
A Musical Joke

Composed by Wolfgang Amadeus Mozart

Theme from Variations in A
K.137

Composed by Wolfgang Amadeus Mozart

Theme from Piano Sonata In C

Composed by Wolfgang Amadeus Mozart

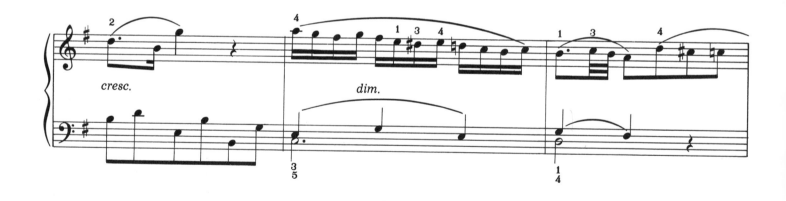

Rondo Alla Turca

Composed by Wolfgang Amadeus Mozart

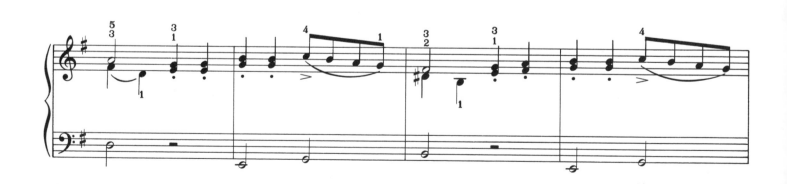

Theme from Piano Concerto In C
K.467

Composed by Wolfgang Amadeus Mozart

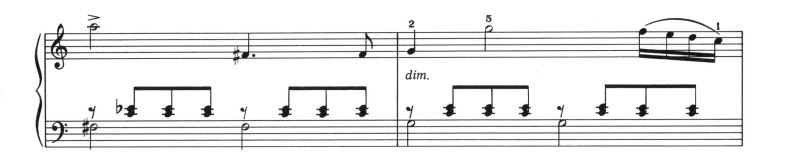

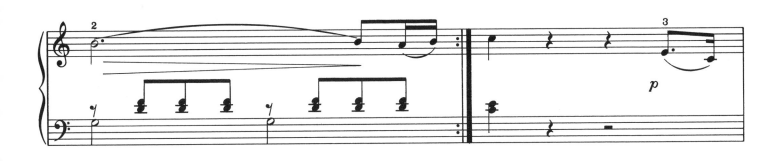

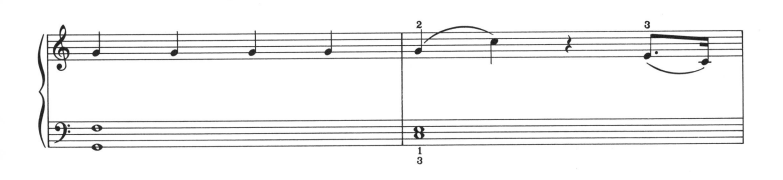

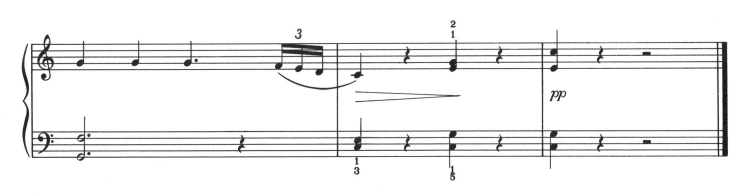

Minuet K.94

Composed by Wolfgang Amadeus Mozart

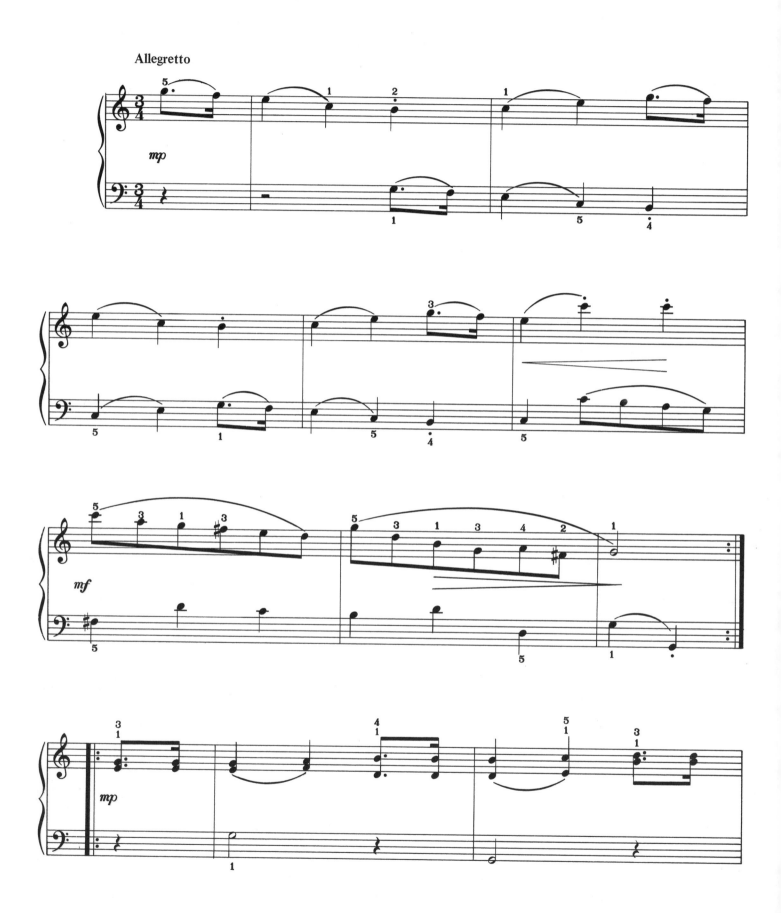

Zerlina's Song from Don Giovanni

Composed by Wolfgang Amadeus Mozart

Now Your Days Of Philandering Are Over

Composed by Wolfgang Amadeus Mozart

Eine Kleine Nachtmusik
(Romance)

Composed by Wolfgang Amadeus Mozart

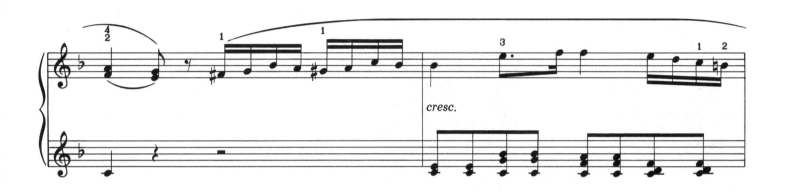

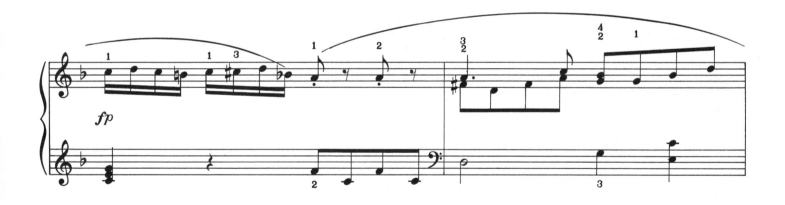

Printed in England by Caligraving Limited Thetford Norfolk

2/07 (61453)

Bringing you the words and the music

All the latest music in print... rock & pop plus jazz, blues, country, classical and the best in West End show scores.

- Books to match your favourite CDs.

- Book-and-CD titles with high quality backing tracks for you to play along to. Now you can play guitar or piano with your favourite artist... or simply sing along!

- Audition songbooks with CD backing tracks for both male and female singers for all those with stars in their eyes.

- Can't read music? No problem, you can still play all the hits with our wide range of chord songbooks.

- Check out our range of instrumental tutorial titles, taking you from novice to expert in no time at all!

- Musical show scores include *The Phantom Of The Opera*, *Les Misérables*, *Mamma Mia* and many more hit productions.

- DVD master classes featuring the techniques of top artists.

Visit your local music shop or, in case of difficulty, contact the Marketing Department, Music Sales Limited, Newmarket Road, Bury St Edmunds, Suffolk, IP33 3YB, UK
marketing@musicsales.co.uk